Pencil Code

A Programming Primer

David Bau

Visit http://pencilcode.net/ to run your programs.

"Creativity takes courage."
- Henri Matisse

Pencil Code is an open-source system
that unites the CoffeeScript language by Jeremy Ashkenas in 2009,
and Iced await/defer extensions created by Maxwell Krohn in 2012,
with the jQuery-turtle plugin developed by the author in 2011,
using the jQuery library invented by John Resig in 2006.
This work is inspired by the beloved LOGO language
created by Seymour Papert and Wally Feurzeig in 1967.

Special thanks to the students in Lincoln Massachusetts,
Beaver Country Day School, and Dorchester McCormack School
who vetted this material.

Post questions, ideas, and bug reports to http://pencilcode.net/group

Fancy Sun illustration contributed by Margaret Z.

Random Tree illustration contributed by Mike Koss.

Cover image by Phil Clements. Back cover image by Vinod Velayudhan.

This book is typeset in Łukasz Dziedzic's 2010 open font Lato
and Paul D. Hunt's 2012 Adobe Source Code Pro.

No Thresholds and No Limits

The aim of this book is to teach you to write programs as you would use a pencil: as an outlet for creativity and as a tool for understanding.

These pages follow a fifty-year tradition of using programming as a liberating educational tool, with no thresholds for beginners, and no limits for experts. Seymour Papert's LOGO is the inspiration. Start with a few lines of code, and progress to writing programs to explore art, mathematics, language, algorithms, simulation, and thought.

The language is CoffeeScript. Although CoffeeScript is a production programming language used by pros, it was chosen here because it has an elegance and simplicity well-suited for beginners. While the first examples make the language look trivial, CoffeeScript has a good notation for all the important ideas: algebraic expressions, lists, loops, functions, objects, and concurrency. As you learn the language, remember that the goal should be not mastery of the syntax, but mastery of the underlying concepts.

Edit and run your programs on pencilcode.net. The site is an experiment in community learning: everything posted is public. Write programs that would be interesting to others. Accounts are free.

As you experiment by building your own ideas, you will find that at first your programs will behave in ways that you do not intend. Details matter, and persistence pays off. If you are patient in adjusting and perfecting your work, you will be rewarded with insight.

Read, think, play, and create something beautiful.

David Bau, 2013

Contents

Part 1

Primer:
100 Little Projects

Contents

Part 2

Appendix:
One Project in Detail

Next Steps

Reference

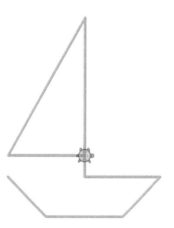

Primer

100 Little Projects

In the following pages, the basic concepts of modern computer programming are shown in a series of brief examples.

None of the examples come with explanations. Just try them.

Once you get a program working, stop and think about how it works. Make your own customized version.

Can you draw a violet with a stem? Can you make a snowflake that really looks like a snowflake? And can you do these things in an elegant way?

For a tutorial introduction to CoffeeScript, turn to the Appendix which begins after example set 26. Also be sure to try the "help" command in the test panel.

Enough advice.

Let's play.

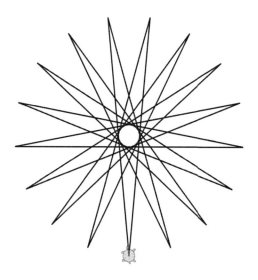

1. Lines

First
```
pen red
fd 50
```

Square
```
pen blue
fd 100
rt 90
fd 100
rt 90
fd 100
rt 90
fd 100
rt 90
```

Triangle
```
pen black
fd 80; rt 120
fd 80; rt 120
fd 80; rt 120
```

House
```
speed 5
pen orange
fd 30; lt 90
fd 10; rt 120
fd 80; rt 120
fd 80; rt 120
fd 10; lt 90
fd 30; rt 90
fd 60; rt 90
```

Turtle
```
pen green
rt 360, 10
lt 45, 30
rt 360, 8
lt 90, 50
rt 360, 8
lt 90, 30
rt 360, 8
lt 90, 50
rt 360, 8
lt 45, 30
```

2. Points

Dot Row

```
rt 90; dot lightgray
fd 30; dot gray
fd 30; dot()
fd 30
```

Message

```
message = 'Hello You.'
see 'message'
see message
```

```
message
Hello You.
```

Lighthouse

```
pen crimson
fd 60; label 'GO'
rt 30
fd 40; rt 120; dot gold, 30
fd 40; rt 30
fd 60; rt 90
fd 40; rt 90
```

Smiley

```
speed 10
dot yellow, 160
fd 20
rt 90
fd 25
dot black, 20
bk 50
dot black, 20
bk 5
rt 90
fd 40
pen black, 7
lt 30
lt 120, 35
ht()
```

Bullseye

```
x = 18
see x * 5
dot black, x * 5
dot white, x * 4
dot black, x * 3
dot white, x * 2
```

90

3. Loops

Rectangle

```
pen green
for d in [50, 100, 50, 100]
  fd d
  rt 90
```

Rainbow

```
for c in [
    red
    orange
    yellow
    green
    blue
    violet
  ]
  pen c
  rt 360, 50
  fd 10
```

Range

```
see [1..5]
see [1...5]
```

```
[1, 2, 3, 4, 5]
[1, 2, 3, 4]
```

Square Loop

```
pen blue
for [1..4]
  fd 100
  rt 90
```

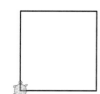

Gold Star

```
pen gold, 3
for [1..5]
  fd 100
  rt 2 * 360 / 5
```

Descending Loop

```
pen purple
for x in [50..1] by -1
  rt 30, x
```

4. Nesting

Violet

```
pen blueviolet
for [1..5]
  rt 72
  for [1..3]
    fd 50
    rt 120
```

Combinations

```
for outside in [skyblue, violet, pink]
  for inside in [palegreen, orange, red]
    dot outside, 21
    dot inside, 7
    fd 25
    rt 36
```

Decorated Nest

```
pen turquoise
for [1..10]
  dot blue
  for [1..4]
    fd 50
    rt 90
  lt 36
  bk 50
```

Catalog

```
speed 100
rt 90
for color in [red, gold, green, blue]
  jump 40, -160
  for sides in [3..6]
    pen path
    for [1..sides]
      fd 100 / sides
      lt 360 / sides
    fill color
    fd 40
```

5. Functions

Scoot Function
```
pen purple
scoot = (x) -> fd 10 * x
rt 90
scoot 7
```

Spike Function
```
spike = (x) ->
  fd x
  label x
  bk x

pen crimson
for n in [1..6]
  spike n * 10
  rt 60
```

Square Function
```
square = (size) ->
  for [1..4]
    fd size
    rt 90

pen red
square 80

jump 15, 15
pen firebrick
square 50
```

Tee Function
```
tee = ->
  fd 50
  rt 90
  bk 25
  fd 50

pen green
tee()
pen gold
tee()
pen black
tee()
```

6. Parameters

Polygon

```
polygon = (c, s, n) ->
  pen c
  for [1..n]
    fd s
    rt 360 / n
  pen null

polygon blue, 70, 5
bk 50
polygon(orange, 25, 6)
```

Rule

```
rule = (sizes) ->
  for x in sizes
    fd x
    bk x
    rt 90; fd 10; lt 90

pen black
rule [50, 10, 20, 10, 50, 10, 20, 10, 50]
```

Starburst

```
starburst = (x, shape) ->
  for z in [1..x]
    shape()
    rt 360 / x
stick = -> fd 30; bk 30

pen deeppink
starburst 3, stick

jump 0, -60
starburst 20, stick

jump 0, -90
starburst 10, -> fd 30; dot blue; bk 30

jump 0, -100
starburst 5, ->
  fd 30
  starburst 7, ->
    fd 10
    bk 10
  bk 30
```

7. Time

Pause

```
speed 100
pen red
for x in [1..20]
  fd 80
  rt 100
  if x is 10
    pause 2
```

Second Hand

```
speed Infinity
advance = ->
  pen lightgray
  bk 100
  rt 5
  pen red
  fd 100
tick advance
```

Countdown

```
seconds = 5
tick ->
  if seconds is 0
    write "Time's up!"
    tick null
  else
    write seconds
    seconds = seconds - 1
```

5
4
3
2
1
Time's up!

Click Draw

```
speed Infinity
pen green

tick ->
  moveto lastclick
```

Move Draw

```
speed Infinity
pen orange

tick 100, ->
  turnto lastmousemove
  fd 1
```

8. Output

Poetry and Song

```
cry = (who, query) ->
  write "Oh #{who}, #{who}!"
  write "#{query} #{who}?"
cry "Romeo", "Wherefore art thou"
cry "kitty", "What did you eat"
play "fc/c/dcz"
```

Oh Romeo, Romeo!
Wherefore art thou
Romeo?
Oh kitty, kitty!
What did you eat kitty?

Imagery

```
url = "http://upload.wikimedia.org/wikipedia" +
      "/commons/6/61/Baby_Gopher_Tortoise.jpg"
write """<center><img src="#{url}" width=100>
    </center>"""
```

Bold Statement

```
n = write "<h1>Notice</h1>"
write """
<p>This long paragraph has
<b>bold</b>, <i>italic</i>,
and <u>underlined</u> text.
Horizontal rule below.</p>
"""
write "<hr>"
write """
<p><a href="//pencilcode.net/">
Link</a> with an &lt;a&gt;.
</p>
"""
n.css
  background: pink
```

Notice

This long paragraph has **bold**,
italic, and underlined text.
Horizontal rule below.

Link with an <a>.

Graffiti

```
n = write "<h1>Notice</h1>"
write """
<p>This long paragraph has
<b>bold</b>, <i>italic</i>,
and <u>underlined</u> text.
</p>"""
n.css
  background: pink
  display: 'inline-block'
n.pen purple, 10
n.bk 80
n.rt 45
n.fd 50
```

This lo... pa... ...has **bold**,
italic, and unde...ined text.

9. Input

Button Control

```
pen sienna
button 'R', -> rt 10
button 'F', -> fd 10
button 'D', -> dot 'darkslateblue'
```

Polygon to Order

```
await read "Color?", defer color
await read "Sides?", defer sides
pen color
for [1..sides]
  fd 30
  rt 360 / sides
```

Color? green
Sides? 8

Guess My Number

```
secret = random [1..100]
turns = 5
write "Guess my number."
while turns > 0
  await readnum defer pick
  if pick is secret
    write "You got it!"
    break
  if 1 <= pick < secret
    write "Too small! "
    turns = turns - 1
  else if secret < pick <= 100
    write "Too big! "
    turns = turns - 1
  if turns > 1
    write "#{turns} left."
  else if turns is 1
    write "Last guess!"
  else
    write "Game over."
    write "It was #{secret}."
    break
```

Guess my number.
⇒ 50
Too small!
4 left.
⇒ 75
Too big!
3 left.
⇒ 64
Too big!
2 left.
⇒ 55
Too small!
Last guess!
⇒ 59
You got it!

Polygon Revisited

```
read "Color?", (color) ->
  read "Sides?", (sides) ->
    pen color
    for [1..sides]
      fd 30
      rt 360 / sides
```

Color? red
Sides? 8

10. Numbers

Parsing

```
write '5' + '3'
write Number('5') + Number('3')
```

53
8

Ways to Count

```
counter = 0
write ++counter + 'a'
write (counter += 1) + 'b'
write (counter = counter + 1) + 'c'
```

1a
2b
3c

Circle Measurements

```
area = (radius) ->
  Math.PI * radius * radius

circumference = (radius) ->
  2 * Math.PI * radius

for r in [1, 5, 10]
  write 'radius ' + r
  write 'a ' + area r
  write 'c ' + circumference r
```

radius 1
a 3.141592653589793
c 6.283185307179586
radius 5
a 78.53981633974483
c 31.41592653589793
radius 10
a 314.1592653589793
c 62.83185307179586

Hypotenuse

```
hypotenuse = (a, b) ->
  Math.sqrt(a * a + b * b)

write hypotenuse 3, 4
write hypotenuse 5, 12
write hypotenuse 10, 10
write Math.floor(hypotenuse(10, 10))
```

5
13
14.142135623730951
14

Euclid's Method

```
gcf = (a, b) ->
  if a > b
    return gcf b, a
  remainder = b % a
  if remainder is 0
    return a
  gcf remainder, a

for x in [80..88]
  write "gcf(120,#{x})=" +
    gcf(120, x)
```

gcf(120,80)=40
gcf(120,81)=3
gcf(120,82)=2
gcf(120,83)=1
gcf(120,84)=12
gcf(120,85)=5
gcf(120,86)=2
gcf(120,87)=3
gcf(120,88)=8

11. Computation

Power

```
power = (x, p) ->
  answer = 1
  answer *= x for i in [0...p]
  return answer
for n in [1..5]
  write power(2, n)
```
```
2
4
8
16
32
```

Built-in Power

```
write Math.pow(2, 5)
write Math.pow(2, 0.5)
```
```
32
1.4142135623730951
```

Factorial

```
factorial = (x) ->
  if x < 1 then 1
  else x * factorial(x - 1)
for x in [1..4]
  write factorial x
```
```
1
2
6
24
```

Fibonacci

```
fib = (n) ->
  if n <= 2
    1
  else
    fib(n - 1) + fib(n - 2)
for x in [3..8]
  write fib x
```
```
2
3
5
8
13
21
```

Complex

```
mandelbrot = (n, c, z) ->
  if n is 0 or z.r*z.r + z.i*z.i > 4
    return n
  else return mandelbrot n - 1, c,
    r: c.r + z.r*z.r - z.i*z.i
    i: c.i + 2*z.r*z.i
speed 100
ht()
scale 150
s = 0.05
for x in [-2..1] by s
  for y in [-1.5..1.5] by s
    n = mandelbrot 20, {r:x,i:y}, {r:x,i:y}
    moveto x, y
    dot hsl(100, 1, n/20), s
```

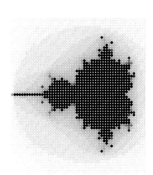

12. Objects

Page Coordinates

```
startpos =
  pageX: 80
  pageY: 10
moveto startpos
pen coral
moveto
  pageX: 30
  pageY: 50
moveto {pageX: 160, pageY: 50}
```

Figure

```
figure = [
  {c: dimgray, x: 75,  y: 12}
  {c: gray,    x: 0,   y: 78}
  {c: dimgray, x: -75, y: 5}
  {c: gray,    x: -35, y: -18}
  {c: plum,    x: 0,   y: -62}
  {c: gray,    x: 35,  y: -15}
  {c: black,   x: 0,   y: 95}
]
for line in figure
  pen line.c
  slide line.x, line.y
```

Scoring

```
points =
  a: 1, e: 1, i: 1, l: 1, n: 1, o: 1, r: 1, s: 1, t: 1, u: 1
  d: 2, g: 2, b: 3, c: 3, m: 3, p: 3, f: 4, h: 4, v: 4, w: 4, y: 4
  k: 5, j: 8, x: 8, q: 10, z: 10
score = (word) ->
  total = 0
  for letter in word
    total += points[letter]
  write "#{word}: #{total}"
score x for x in ['bison', 'armadillo', 'giraffe', 'zebra']
```

```
bison: 7
armadillo: 12
giraffe: 14
zebra: 16
```

Methods

```
memo =
  sum: 0
  count: 0
  add: (x) -> @sum += x; @count += 1
  stats: ->
    write "Total #{this.sum} / #{this.count}"
    write "Average #{this.sum / this.count}"
memo.add(n) for n in [40..50]
memo.stats()
```

```
Total 495 / 11
Average 45
```

13. Arrays

Story

```
story = [
  'Exclamation?'
  '!  he said '
  'adverb?'
  ' as he jumped into his convertible '
  'noun?'
  ' and drove off with his '
  'adjective?'
  ' wife.'
]
for i in [0...story.length] by 2
  prompt = story[i]
  await read prompt, defer answer
  story[i] = answer
write story.join ''
```

Exclamation? Yowzer
adverb? slowly
noun? [   ]

Primes

```
primes = []
candidate = 2
while primes.length < 10
  composite = false
  for p in primes
    if candidate % p is 0
      composite = true
      break
  if not composite
    primes.push candidate
    write candidate
  candidate = candidate + 1
```

2
3
5
7
11
13
17
19
23
29

Push and Pop

```
stack = []
pen green
speed Infinity
button 'R', -> rt 30
button 'F', -> fd 10
button 'Push', ->
  dot crimson
  stack.push [getxy(), direction()]
button 'Pop', ->
  if not stack.length then home(); return
  [xy, b] = stack.pop()
  jumpto xy
  turnto b
  dot pink
```

R F Push Pop

14. Recursion

Recursive Spiral

```
spiral = (x) ->
  if x > 0
    fd x * 10
    rt 90
    spiral x - 1
    lt 90
    bk x * 10
pen red
spiral 10
```

Fractal Fern

```
speed 1000
fern = (x) ->
  if x > 1
    fd x
    rt 95
    fern x * .4
    lt 190
    fern x * .4
    rt 100
    fern x * .8
    lt 5
    bk x
pen green
fern 50
```

Koch Snowflake

```
speed Infinity
flake = (x) ->
  if x < 3 then fd x
  else
    flake x / 3
    lt 60
    flake x / 3
    rt 120
    flake x / 3
    lt 60
    flake x / 3
pen 'path'
for [1..3]
  flake 150
  rt 120
fill 'azure strokeStyle navy'
```

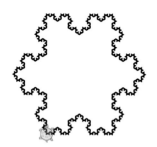

15. Randomness

Two Dice

```
onedice = ->
  random [1..6]
twodice = ->
  onedice() + onedice()
for [1..5]
  write twodice()
```

6
9
11
8
10

Random Walk

```
for [1..20]
  fd 10
  rt random(181) - 90
  dot gray, 5
```

Cubism

```
for [1..14]
  pen random [red,black,blue]
  fd random 70
  rt 90
```

Confetti

```
for [1..300]
  moveto random position
  dot random color
```

Decimal Random

```
for [1..2]
  write Math.random()
```

0.3955826204144705
0.46279336348825273

Five Flips

```
c = [0, 0, 0, 0, 0, 0]
for [1..500]
  heads = 0
  for [1..5]
    heads += random 2
  c[heads] += 1
for h of c
  b = write h + ":" + c[h]
  b.css
    background: skyblue
    width: c[h]
```

0:21
1:73
2:160
3:145
4:85
5:16

16. Sets

Scatter

```
turtle.remove()
s = hatch 15, orange
s.pen gold
s.plan ->
  this.rt random 360
  this.fd Math.abs(20 * random normal)
```

Turtle Race

```
fd 200; pen red; slide 200, 0
finished = 0
racers = hatch 7
racers.plan (j) ->
  @wear random color
  @speed 5 + random normal
  @slide j * 25 + 25, 0
  while not @touches red
    @fd random 5
    await @done defer()
  @label ++finished
```

Rescue Class

```
turtle.remove()
speed 100
randpos = ->
  [50 * random(normal), 50 * random(normal)]
hatch(20, green).scale(0.75).plan ->
  this.moveto randpos()
  this.addClass 'kid'
hatch(3, red).plan (num) ->
  hero = this
  count = 0
  hero.moveto randpos()
  hero.pen red
  while true
    await hero.done defer()
    kid = $('.kid').nearest(hero).eq(0)
    if kid.length is 0
      write "hero ##{num} got #{count}"
      return
    else if hero.touches(kid)
      count += 1
      kid.label num
      kid.remove()
    else
      hero.turnto(kid).fd(5)
```

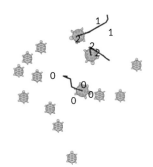

17. Text

```
text = """"If you can look into the seeds of time
            And say which grain will grow and which will not,
            Speak, then, to me."""
```

Substr
```
see text.indexOf 'which'                          47
see text.substr 47, 7                             which g
```

Unicode
```
see 'charCode', text.charCodeAt(0)                charCode 73
see 'string', String.fromCharCode(73)             string I
for x in [88, 188, 9988]                          88 X
  see x, String.fromCharCode(x)                    188 ¼
                                                   9988 ✂
```

Match
```
see text.match /w....g.../                        ["will grow"]
see text.match /[a-z][a-z]/                        ["yo"]
see text.match /\s[a-z][a-z]\s/                    [" of "]
see text.match /\b[a-z][a-z]\b/                    ["of"]
see text.match /\b[a-z][a-z]\b/gi                  ["If", "of", "to", "me"]
see text.match /\b[gn][a-z]*\b/g                   ["grain", "grow", "not"]
see text.match /z/                                 null
```

Split
```
lines = text.split /\n/                            Speak, then, to me.
see lines[2]                                       ["If", "you", "can"]
words = text.split /\s+/
see words[0..2]
```

Groups
```
pattern = /\b([a-z]+) of ([a-z]+)\b/               group 0: seeds of time
matched = pattern.exec text                        group 1: seeds
for g in [0..2]                                     group 2: time
  see "group #{g}: #{matched[g]}"
```

Replace
```
r = text.replace /[A-Z][a-z]*/g,
    "<mark>$&</mark>"
r = r.replace /\n/g,
    "<br>"
r = r.replace /\bw[a-z]*\b/g,
    (x) -> x.toUpperCase()
write r
```

If you can look into the
seeds of time
And say WHICH grain
WILL grow and WHICH
WILL not,
Speak, then, to me.

18. Motion

Bounce

```
speed Infinity
pen purple
vy = 10
tick 20, ->
  slide 1, vy
  if inside(window)
    vy -= 1
  else
    vy = Math.abs(vy) * 0.9
```

Tag

```
speed Infinity
write "Catch blue!"
b = hatch blue
bk 100
tick 10, ->
  turnto lastmousemove
  fd 5
  b.turnto 45 + direction b
  b.fd 6
  if b.touches(turtle)
    write "You win!"
    tick off
  else if not b.touches(window)
    write "Blue got away!"
    tick off
```

Catch blue!

Orbit

```
speed Infinity; pen orange
G = 100
v = [0, 1]
sun = hatch(gold)
sun.slide G, 0
tick 100, ->
  sun.moveto lastclick
  s = sun.getxy()
  p = getxy()
  d = distance(sun)
  d3 = d * d * d
  if d3 > 0 then for i in [0..1]
    v[i] += G * (s[i] - p[i]) / d3
  slide v[0], v[1]
```

19. Concurrency

Race Condition
```
b = hatch blue
r = hatch red
b.lt 90; b.pen blue
b.play 'g'
b.rt 170, 50
b.dot 50, blue
r.rt 90; r.pen red
r.play 'd'
r.lt 170, 50
r.dot 50, red
```

Line Follower
```
dot orange, 220
dot white, 180
jump 100, 0
pen skyblue
while true
  fd 3 + random 3
  await done defer()
  if touches orange
    lt 5
  else
    rt 5
```

Shared Memory
```
shared = { d: 0 }
do ->
  while true
    await read defer shared.d
do ->
  pen red
  while true
    fd 10
    await done defer()
    rt shared.d
```

⇒ 30
⇒ -20
⇒ [   ]

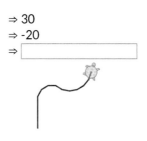

Message Passing
```
button 'send color', ->
  send 'go', random color
do ->
  for x in [1..25]
    await recv 'go', defer c
    pen c
    fd 50
    rt 88, 10
```

send color

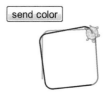

Thick Lines

```
pen blue, 10
fd 100; rt 90
pen pink, 3
fd 50; rt 90
pen 'orange ' +
    'lineWidth 10 ' +
    'lineCap square'
fd 100; rt 90
pen black
fd 50
```

Border

```
text = write 'Outlined.'
text.css { border: '2px solid red' }
turtle.css { border: '3px dotted blue' }
```

Font

```
h = write 'Fancy!'
h.css
  font: '55px Helvetica'
  fontStyle: 'italic'
```

Fancy!

Text Decoration

```
write 'Before'
d = write 'Decorated'
write 'After'
d.css
  display: 'inline-block'
  cursor: 'pointer'
  padding: '10px'
  margin: '-5px'
  opacity: '0.7'
  color: 'white'
  fontSize: '110%'
  letterSpacing: '5px'
  textDecoration: 'underline'
  boxShadow: '1px 1px black'
  background: 'mediumaquamarine'
  transform: 'rotate(10deg)translateX(20px)'
```

Before

After

21. Selectors

Tags

```
write """<style>
h2 { color: red; }
h3 { background: bisque; }
</style>
"""
write "<h2>Stylesheet</h2>"
write "<h3>Tag Styles</h3>"
write "<h3>style specific tags</h3>"
```

Stylesheet

Tag Styles

style specific tags

Classes

```
write """
<style>
.a { text-decoration: underline; }
.b { font-style: italic; }
</style>
"""
write "<p class='a'>Class a</p>"
write "<h3 class='b'>Class b</h3>"
write "<p class='b'>Classes apply to any tag.</p>"
```

<u>Class a</u>

Class b

Classes apply to any tag.

Composites

```
write """
<style>
i { border: 1px solid black; margin: 2px;
    display:inline-table }
i:nth-of-type(1) { background: gold }
i:nth-of-type(2n+4) { background: skyblue }
i:nth-of-type(3n+9) { background: thistle }
</style>
"""
for x in [1..24]
  write "<i>#{x}</i>"
```

1 2 3 4 5 6 7 8 9 10 11
12 13 14 15 16 17 18 19
20 21 22 23 24

jQuery

```
write "<p><mark>a</mark>v<mark>o</mark>" +
      "c<mark>a</mark>d<mark>o</mark></p>"
$('p').css { fontSize: '200%' }
$('mark').css { background: palegreen }
$('mark').animate {
  padding: '5px' }
$('mark:nth-of-type(2n)').animate {
  opacity: 0.3 }
```

a v o c a d o

22. Events

Shift Click

```
$(document).click (event) ->
  see event
  if event.shiftKey
    pen blue
  else
    pen null
  moveto event
```

Arrow Keys

```
pen plum
[L, R, U, D] = [37, 39, 38, 40]
keydown (event) ->
  if event.which is L then lt 5
  if event.which is R then rt 5
  if event.which is U then fd 5
  if event.which is D then bk 5
```

Can't Touch This

```
t = write "<button>Touch This</button>"
t.speed Infinity
t.moveto document
t.mousemove (event) ->
  t.rt random(91) - 45
  while t.touches(event)
    t.bk 1
```

Magic Hat

```
speed Infinity
turtle.remove()
t = write '<img>'
t.home()
start = ->
  t.wear 'openicon:magic-tophat'
  tick off
  t.click (event) -> play()
play = ->
  t.wear 'openicon:animals-rabbit'
  tick ->
    t.moveto random 'position'
  t.click (event) -> start()
start()
```

23. Slicing

Choices

```
choices = (menu, sofar = []) ->
  if menu.length is 0
    write sofar.join ' '
  else for item in menu[0]
    choices menu[1...],
      sofar.concat item

choices [
  ['small', 'medium', 'large']
  ['vanilla', 'chocolate']
  ['cone', 'cup']
]
```

small vanilla cone
small vanilla cup
small chocolate cone
small chocolate cup
medium vanilla cone
medium vanilla cup
medium chocolate cone
medium chocolate cup
large vanilla cone
large vanilla cup
large chocolate cone
large chocolate cup

Shuffle

```
suits = ['\u2663', '\u2666', '\u2665', '\u2660']
deck = []
for v in [2..10].concat ['J', 'Q', 'K', 'A']
  deck.push (v + s for s in suits)...
shuffle = (d) ->
  for i in [1...d.length]
    choice = random(i + 1)
    [d[i], d[choice]] = [d[choice], d[i]]
deal = (d, n) -> d.splice(-n)

shuffle deck
for [1..3]
  write deal(deck, 5).join('/')
```

J♦/3♠/7♣/9♥/6♠
3♥/10♦/7♥/7♦/8♥
A♦/Q♥/2♣/8♠/K♦

Caesar Cipher

```
key = 13
a2z = 'ABCDEFGHIJKLMNOPQRSTUVWXYZ'
rot = a2z[key...].concat a2z[...key]
box = write '<input>'
out = write ''

box.keyup ->
  result = for c in box.val()
    char = c.toUpperCase()
    if char in a2z
      rot[a2z.indexOf char]
    else
      char
  out.text result.join ''
```

attack at dawn
NGGNPX NG QNJA

24. Sorting

Quick Sort

```
list = (random 10 for [1..8])
list.sort()
write list
```

3,4,4,5,6,7,7,8

Slow Selection Sort

```
show = (points, highlight) ->
  render = for k, v of points
    if Number(k) in highlight
      "<mark>#{v}</mark>"
    else
      "#{v}"
  write "<div>#{render.join ','}</div>"

list = 'SORTME'.split ''
show list, []

for i in [0 ... list.length - 1]
  for j in [i + 1 ... list.length]
    if list[i] > list[j]
      [list[i], list[j]] =
        [list[j], list[i]]
    show list, [i, j]
```

S,O,R,T,M,E
O,S,R,T,M,E
O,S,R,T,M,E
O,S,R,T,M,E
M,S,R,T,O,E
E,S,R,T,O,M
E,R,S,T,O,M
E,R,S,T,O,M
E,O,S,T,R,M
E,M,S,T,R,O
E,M,S,T,R,O
E,M,R,T,S,O
E,M,O,T,S,R
E,M,O,S,T,R
E,M,O,R,T,S
E,M,O,R,S,T

Custom Quick Sort

```
sketch = (points) ->
  cg()
  pen null
  for p in points
    moveto p
    pen red
    dot black

array = []

button 'scatter', ->
  array = for [1..10]
    random 'position'
  sketch array

button 'sort',  ->
  array.sort (a, b) ->
    a.pageX - b.pageX
  sketch array
```

scatter sort

25. Search

Maze

```
[width, height] = [9, 9]
grid = table(width, height).home()

sides = [
  {dx: 0, dy: -1, ob: 'borderTop', ib: 'borderBottom'}
  {dx: 1, dy: 0, ob: 'borderRight', ib: 'borderLeft'}
  {dx: 0, dy: 1, ob: 'borderBottom', ib: 'borderTop'}
  {dx: -1, dy: 0, ob: 'borderLeft', ib: 'borderRight'}
]

isopen = (x, y, side) ->
  return /none/.test(
    grid.cell(y, x).css side.ob)

isbox = (x, y) ->
  return false unless (
    0 <= x < width and
    0 <= y < height)
  for s in sides
    if isopen x, y, s
      return false
  return true

makemaze = (x, y) ->
  loop
    adj = (s for s in sides when isbox x + s.dx, y + s.dy)
    if adj.length is 0 then return
    choice = random adj
    [nx, ny] = [x + choice.dx, y + choice.dy]
    grid.cell(y, x).css choice.ob, 'none'
    grid.cell(ny, nx).css choice.ib, 'none'
    makemaze nx, ny

wander = (x, y, lastdir) ->
  moveto grid.cell y, x
  for d in [lastdir + 3 .. lastdir + 7]
    dir = d % 4
    s = sides[dir]
    if isopen x, y, s then break
  turnto grid.cell y + s.dy, x + s.dx unless dir is lastdir
  plan -> wander x + s.dx, y + s.dy, dir

makemaze 0, 0
speed 5
wander 4, 4, 0
```

26. Intelligence

Tic Tac Toe

```
grid = table 3, 3,
  {width: 48, height: 48, font: "32px Arial Black", background: "wheat"}
grid.home()
board = [0, 0, 0,   0, 0, 0,   0, 0, 0]

grid.cell().click ->
  move = grid.cell().index this
  return unless winner() is 0 and board[move] is 0
  board[move] = 1
  $(this).text 'X'
  setTimeout respond, 500

respond = ->
  response = bestmove(-1).move
  if response?
    board[response] = -1;
    grid.cell().eq(response).text 'O'
  colorwinner()

bestmove = (player) ->
  win = winner()
  if win isnt 0 then return {move: null, advantage: win}
  choices = {'-1': [], '0': [], '1': []}
  for think in [0..8] when board[think] is 0
    board[think] = player
    outcome = bestmove(-player).advantage
    choices[outcome].push {move: think, advantage: outcome}
    board[think] = 0
  for favorite in [player, 0, -player] when choices[favorite].length
    return random choices[favorite]
  return {move: null, advantage: 0}

rules = [[0,1,2],[3,4,5],[6,7,8],[0,3,6],[1,4,7],[2,5,8],[0,4,8],[2,4,6]]

winner = ->
  for row in rules
    if board[row[0]] and board[row[0]] is board[row[1]] is board[row[2]]
      return board[row[0]]
  return 0

colorwinner = ->
  for row in rules
    if board[row[0]] and board[row[0]] is board[row[1]] is board[row[2]]
      for n in row
        grid.cell().eq(n).css {color: red}
```

Appendix

Hangman
One Project in Detail

In this section, we use Pencil Code to make a game of hangman from scratch.

It takes a couple hours to learn enough programming to make a game of hangman.

We will learn about:

- Memory and naming
- Computer arithmetic
- Using functions
- Simple graphics
- How to make a program
- Input and output
- Loops and choices
- Delays and synchronization
- Connecting to the internet

At the end we will have a game we can play.

1. Running Pencil Code

Go to pencilcode.net.

Click on "Let's Play!"

The screen should look like this:

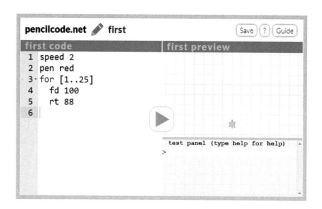

The left side of the screen is where you type in your program, and the right is where programs run. The lower right corner is a test panel where you type code and run it right away.

While exploring the projects in this book, you can also use the test panel in the lower right corner to ask for help with how commands work.

```
   test panel (type help for help)
 > help
   help is available for: bk cg cs ct fd ht if ln lt rt st abs cos dot
   ...
 >
```

The characters that you should type will be highlighted.

Press Enter after you type **help**.

2. Keeping a Secret

We will begin by working in the test panel.

CoffeeScript can remember things. Let's tell it a secret word.

Type the blue words below into the test panel.

```
test panel (type help for help)
> secret = 'crocodile'
```

See what happens when you press Enter.

```
test panel (type help for help)
> secret = 'crocodile'
  "crocodile"
>
```

Reveal your secret by typing "write secret".

```
> write secret
>
```

Check the upper right panel!

Typing just the name in the test panel will reveal the word there.

```
> secret
  "crocodile"
>
```

Now try something CoffeeScript doesn't know. Try typing "number".

```
> number
  ►number is not defined
>
```

Don't worry. This is fine. You just need to teach CoffeeScript what "number" is and try again.

```
> number = 43
  43
> number
  43
>
```

3. Computers are Fine Calculators

A computer is better than any calculator at doing math. Let's try.

```
> 2+33+66
  101
```

In CoffeeScript, plus and minus use the usual symbols + and −. Times and divide are done using the * and / symbol.

```
> 33333333 * 44444444 / 22
  67340065993266
```

Named values can be used in formulas.

```
> n=123456789
  123456789
> n*n*n
  1.8816763717891548e+24
```

The e+24 at the end is the way that large numbers are written in CoffeeScript. It means $1.8816763717891548 \times 10^{24}$. CoffeeScript calculates numbers with 15 digits of precision.

There are several ways to change a number. For example, += changes a variable by adding to it.

```
> n += 1
  123456790
> n
  123456790
>
```

Some symbols to know:

code	meaning	code	meaning	code	meaning
+	plus	x = 95	save 95 as x	'a' in word	does the word contain an 'a'?
−	minus	x is 24	is x equal to 24?	String(num)	turns num into a string of digits
*	times	x < 24	is x less than 24?	Number(digits)	makes a number from a string
/	divide	x > 24	is x more than 24?	n += 1	change n by adding one

These operations can be combined.

CoffeeScript obeys the same order of operations used in Algebra.

What will it say for `(2 * 3 + 3 * 5) / 7 − 1`?

What will it do when we try `'7' in String(99 * 123)`?

Try your own fancy formulas. Don't worry if you get errors.

4. Strings and Numbers

What do you think happens when we try to do addition with words?

```
> 'dog' + 'cat'
  dogcat
> 'dog' + 5
  dog5
> 34 + 5
  39
> '34' + 5
  345
>
```

When we put something inside quotes, CoffeeScript treats it like a string of letters, even if it is all digits! That is why '34' + 5 is 345. Quoted values like this are called "strings."

The Number() function can be used to convert a string to a number, so that we can do ordinary arithmetic with it.

The String() function is opposite, and turns numbers into strings.

```
> Number('34') + 5
  39
> String(34) + 5
  345
> Number('dog') + 5
  NaN
>
```

If we try to convert a string to a number in a way that does not make sense, we get NaN, which stands for "Not a Number".

5. Creating Graphics

In Pencil Code, we can create graphics by using the turtle. There are five basic turtle functions:

code	meaning
pen red	chooses the pen color red
fd 100	moves forward by 100 pixels
rt 90	turns right by 90 degrees
lt 120	turns left by 120 degrees
bk 50	slides back by 50 pixels

In the test panel, enter two commands to draw a line:

```
> pen red
> fd 50
>
```

The reference at the end of this book lists many other colors that can be used. To stop drawing, use "pen null" to select no pen.

Try turning the turtle and drawing another line. Notice that rt turns the turtle in place, and we need to move the turtle with fd to draw a corner.

```
...
> rt 90
> fd 100
>
```

Read about the *rt* function using *help*:

```
> help rt
  rt(degrees) Right turn. Pivots clockwise by some degrees: rt 90
  rt(degrees, radius) Right arc. Pivots with a turning radius:
       rt 90, 50
>
```

If we give a second number to *rt*, the turtle will move while turning and form an arc. Try making a circle:

```
...
> rt 360, 30
>
```

Remember to put a comma between the two numbers.

6. Making our First Program

We are ready to set up a hangman game. In the the editor on the left side of Pencil Code:

- Select and erase the example program text in the editor.
- Now type the following program into the editor.

```
pen blue
fd 150
rt 90
fd 50
rt 90
fd 20
```

Press the triangular play button!

If it doesn't work, check the typing carefully and try again. Things to watch out for:

- Spell each function name correctly and in lowercase.
- Do not indent any of the lines of this program.
- Remember to put a space after the function names.

Each time we run the program, it clears the screen and starts again.

Now, rename the program from "first" to "hangman" by editing the name next to the pencil. Save it with the button at the top right.

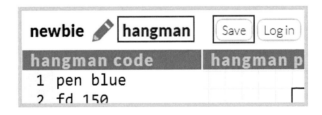

A website will be created with your account name. If I choose the account name "newbie," a website is created at "newbie.pencilcode.net".

Once you have saved the program with the name "hangman," it is available at two different addresses on pencilcode:

- http://*yourname*.pencilcode.net/*edit*/hangman - this is where anyone can see and edit your program, but you need your password to save any changes.
- http://*yourname*.pencilcode.net/*home*/hangman - here is where you can share and run your program without showing the code.

7. Hurry Up and Wait

Write a welcome message after drawing the hangman shape:

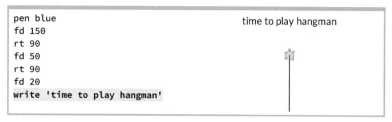

```
pen blue
fd 150
rt 90
fd 50
rt 90
fd 20
write 'time to play hangman'
```

Notice that the Pencil Code Turtle is as slow as a turtle! Unless we speed it up with the *speed* function, the turtle takes its own slow time long after we have asked it to move, and the welcome message appears before the turtle is finished.

We can do two things to help with the slow turtle:
- Change the number of moves it makes per second using "*speed*."
- Ask the program to wait for the turtle, using "*await* done defer()."

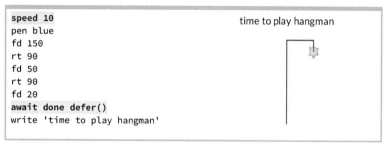

```
speed 10
pen blue
fd 150
rt 90
fd 50
rt 90
fd 20
await done defer()
write 'time to play hangman'
```

Now the turtle moves faster, and the program waits until the turtle is done before writing the welcome message.

A couple things to know:
- Do not use a space between *defer* and the parentheses "defer()".
- We can make the turtle move instantly by using "speed Infinity".

Even if you have programmed before, await/defer may be new to you. These keywords create **continuations**, and they are part of Iced CoffeeScript. To explore how they work in more detail, look up Max Krohn's Iced CoffeeScript page online.

8. Using "for" to Repeat

We can repeat steps in a program with the "for" command.

Try adding three lines to the end of our program so that it looks like this:

```
write 'time to play hangman'
secret = 'crocodile'
for letter in secret
  write letter
```

You should see this:

```
time to play hangman
c
r
o
c
o
d
i
l
e
```

The program is saying: for every letter in the secret, write letter. So the computer repeats "write letter" nine times, once for each letter.

If it doesn't work, check the program and make sure the line after the *for* is indented; that is how CoffeeScript knows which line to repeat.

Once you have the hang of it, keep the word secret by changing the program to write underscores instead of letters:

```
write 'time to play hangman'
for letter in secret
  append '_ '
```

Notice how "*append*" instead of "*write*" puts text on the same line instead of starting a new line each time:

```
time to play hangman
_ _ _ _ _ _ _ _ _
```

9. Using "if" to Choose

In our hangman game, we should show where any guessed letters are. To decide whether to print a blank line or a letter, we will need to use "if" and "else".

Add four new lines to our program:

```
write 'time to play hangman'
secret = 'crocodile'
show = 'aeiou'

for letter in secret
  if letter in show
    append letter + ' '
  else
    append '_ '
```

Don't forget to line everything up, and remember to save it.

What happens when you run it? It reveals all the letters in "show": all the vowels.

Our screen looks like this:

```
time to play hangman
_ _ o _ o _ i _ e
```

Here is how it works.

The line "*if* letter in show" makes a choice.
- If the letter is among our shown, it appends the letter together with a space after it.
- Otherwise ("else") it appends a little underscore with a space after it.

Since the whole thing is indented under the "*for* letter in secret," this choice is repeated for every letter.

Check the spelling and spacing and punctuation if you get errors. Take your time to get it to work.

10. Input with "read"

Our game is no good if players can't guess. To let the player guess, type:

It works like this:

```
await read defer guess
```

"read" opens an input box and collects the input.

The "await" and "defer" commands work together to make the program wait until the read function is done.

"guess" is the name of the input collected by "read".

Try adding these lines to the program:

```
write 'time to play hangman'
secret = 'crocodile'
show = 'aeiou'
write 'guess a letter'
await read defer guess
show += guess
for letter in secret
  if letter in show
    append letter + ' '
  else
    append '_ '
```

Adding "write 'guess a letter'" will let the player know when to enter a guess.

The "show += guess" line adds the guess to the string of shown letters.

Let's run it.

```
time to play hangman
guess a letter
⇒ c
c _ o _ o _ i _ e
```

When we run the program, it will show us where our guessed letter appears.

11. Using "while" to Repeat

We need to let the player take more than one turn.

"while turns > 0" repeats everything indented under it while the player still has turns left.

```
write 'time to play hangman'
secret = 'crocodile'
show = 'aeiou'
turns = 5

while turns > 0
    for letter in secret
        if letter in show
            append letter + ' '
        else
            append '_ '

    write 'guess a letter'
    await read defer guess
    show += guess
    turns -= 1
```

Indent everything under the "while" command to make this work.

The editor will indent a whole block of code if you select it all at once and press the "Tab" key on the keyboard. "Shift-Tab" will unident code.

"turns -= 1" means subtract one from "turns". It will count down each time the player guesses. When "turns" is finally zero, the "while" command will stop repeating.

Try running the program. Does it work?

Any time we want to see the value of a variable, we can type its name into the test panel.

```
    test panel (type help for help)
>  show
    aeioucsn
>  turns
    2
>  ▊
```

How would you give the player more guesses?

12. Improving our Game

We can already play our game. Now we should fix it up to make it fun.

- The player should win right away when there are no missing letters.
- The player should only lose a turn on a wrong guess.
- When the player loses, the game should tell the secret.

Try this:

```
write 'time to play hangman'
secret = 'crocodile'
show = 'aeiou'
turns = 5

while turns > 0
  blanks = 0
  for letter in secret
    if letter in show
      append letter + ' '
    else
      append '_ '
      blanks += 1

  if blanks is 0
    write 'You win!'
    break

  write 'guess a letter'
  await read defer guess
  show += guess

  if guess not in secret
    turns -= 1
    write 'Nope.'
    write turns + ' more turns'
    if turns is 0
      write 'The answer is ' + secret
```

Each time the word is printed, the "blanks" number starts at zero and counts up the number of blanks. If it ends up at zero, it means there are no blanks. So the player has guessed every letter and has won! In that case, the "break" command breaks out of the "while" section early, even though there are still turns left.

The "if guess not in secret" line checks if the guess was wrong. We only count down the "turns" if our guess was wrong.

When we guess wrong, we also print a bunch of messages like "Nope" and how many more turns we have. When we are wrong for the last time we print the secret.

13. Making it Look Like Hangman

It will be more fun if we make our game look like Hangman.

All we need to do is draw parts of the poor hangman person when there is a wrong guess. Try adding something like this to the wrong guess part:

```
...
write 'Nope.'
write turns + ' more turns'
if turns is 4 then lt 90; rt 540, 10; lt 90
if turns is 3 then fd 20; lt 45; bk 30; fd 30
if turns is 2 then rt 90; bk 30; fd 30; lt 45; fd 30
if turns is 1 then rt 45; fd 30
if turns is 1 then fd 30
if turns is 0
  bk 30; lt 90; fd 30
  await done defer()
  write 'The answer is ' + secret
```

The semicolons (;) let you put more than one step on the same line. Notice when putting the "if" on the same line as the commands to run, we must use the word "then" between the test and the commands.

Try making variations on the hangman drawings for each step.

Whenever we want to pause the program to wait for the turtle to finish drawing, we can use "await done defer()".

14. Picking a Random Secret

The only problem with the game is that it always plays the same secret word. We should use the *random* function to choose a random word.

Change the line that sets the secret so that it looks like this:

```
...
write 'time to play hangman'
secret = random ['tiger', 'panda', 'mouse']
show = 'aeiou'
...
```

The square brackets [ ] and commas make a list, and the random function picks one thing randomly from the list.

Of course, we can make the list as long as we like. Here is a longer list:

```
...
write 'time to play hangman'
secret = random [
  'crocodile'
  'elephant'
  'penguin'
  'pelican'
  'leopard'
  'hamster'
]
...
```

The brackets do not have to be on the same line, but we do need two! When we list items on their own lines, the commas are optional.

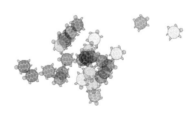

15. Loading a List from the Internet

There is a longer list of animals on the internet at the address
http://pencilcode.net/data/animals.

We can load this data using a jQuery function "$.get". (Read more about
jQuery at learn.jquery.com.)

The code looks like this:

```
...
write 'time to play hangman'
await $.get 'http://pencilcode.net/data/animals', defer animals
secret = random animals.split '\n'
...
```

What this means is:

```
await $.get 'http://pencilcode.net/data/animals', defer animals
```
Pause the program until the $.get is done.

```
await $.get 'http://pencilcode.net/data/animals', defer animals
```
Open up the address http://pencilcode.net/data/animals

```
await $.get 'http://pencilcode.net/data/animals', defer animals
```
Tell $.get to resume the program after putting the answer in "animals."

```
secret = random animals.split '\n'
```
The special string '\n' is the newline character between lines in a file.
Notice that the "\" is a backslash, not the ordinary slash.

```
secret = random animals.split '\n'
```
Split the animals string into an array, with one entry per line.

```
secret = random animals.split '\n'
```
Choose one item from the array randomly.

```
secret = random animals.split '\n'
```
Call this random word "secret".

16. The Whole Hangman Program

Here is the whole program from beginning to end:

```
speed 10
pen blue
fd 150
rt 90
fd 50
rt 90
fd 20
await done defer()
write 'time to play hangman'
await $.get 'http://pencilcode.net/data/animals', defer animals
secret = random animals.split '\n'
show = 'aeiou'
turns = 5

while turns > 0
  blanks = 0
  for letter in secret
    if letter in show
      append letter + ' '
    else
      append '_ '
      blanks += 1

  if blanks is 0
    write 'You win!'
    break

  write 'guess a letter'
  await read defer guess
  show += guess

  if guess not in secret
    turns -= 1
    write 'Nope.'
    write turns + ' more turns'
    if turns is 4 then lt 90; rt 540, 10; lt 90
    if turns is 3 then fd 20; lt 45; bk 30; fd 30
    if turns is 2 then rt 90; bk 30; fd 30; lt 45; fd 30
    if turns is 1 then rt 45; fd 30
    if turns is 0
      bk 30; lt 90; fd 30
      await done defer()
      write 'The answer is ' + secret
```

17. Making it Yours

The best part of programming is adding your own personal style.

Try making the game so that it plays again automatically after you are done. Can you make the game harder or easier? Can you give the player a reward for winning?

Be sure to explore the functions in the online help, and experiment with the examples in the remainder of this book.

For example, you can add sound effects and music. Try exploring the "play" function, and search the internet to learn about ABC notation, chords, waveforms, and ADSR envelopes.

Sometimes the simplest ideas can make a big difference. The "ct()" function clears the text on the screen and the "cg()" function clears the graphics. Maybe this could be used to make a two-player game where one person comes up with the secret word, or where two players compete to guess the word first.

You will soon find that the real fun of programming is in putting your imagination into the code.

Next Steps

Here are a few other places to go to learn more.

Learn more about programming in CoffeeScript with the book Smooth CoffeeScript, by E. Hoigaard (based on the book Eloquent JavaScript, by Marijn Haverbeke).

The await and defer keywords are explained well on Max Krohn's Iced CoffeeScript homepage (search on Google).

The website guide.pencilcode.net has more example programs and reference material to use with Pencil Code.

Pencil Code is based on open web standards HTML5 and CSS3. HTML is a rich subject. There are more than 100 types of HTML elements, more than 100 HTML attributes, more than 100 CSS properties, and an expanding set of standard functions. The best way to explore all these options is to search on Google and consult the many books and resources on the Internet about these standards.

Pencil Code is also built on jQuery, which is the most popular open-source AJAX library for building browser-based web applications. Every turtle is a jQuery object, and a Pencil Code program can use $. Learn about jQuery at learn.jquery.com.

When you have further questions, turn to the Pencil Code discussion group at pencilcode.net/group, or look to the superb technical community on StackOverflow at stackoverflow.com.

Reference

Movement

fd 50	forward 50 pixels
bk 10	backward 10 pixels
rt 90	turn right 90 degrees
lt 120	turn left 120 degrees
home()	go to the page center
slide x, y	slide right x and forward y
moveto x, y	go to x, y relative to home
turnto 45	set direction to 45 (NE)
turnto obj	point toward obj
speed 30	do 30 moves per second

Drawing

pen blue	draw in blue
pen red, 9	9 pixel wide red pen
pen null	use no color
pen off	pause use of the pen
pen on	use the pen again
mark 'X'	mark with an X
dot green	draw a green dot
dot gold, 30	30 pixel gold circle
pen 'path'	trace an invisible path
fill cyan	fill traced path in cyan

Appearance

ht()	hide the turtle
st()	show the turtle
scale 8	do everything 8x bigger
wear yellow	wear a yellow shell
fadeOut()	fade and hide the turtle
remove()	totally remove the turtle

Properties

turtle	name of the main turtle
getxy()	[x, y] position relative to home
direction()	direction of turtle
hidden()	if the turtle is hidden
touches(obj)	if the turtle touches obj
inside(window)	if enclosed in the window
lastmousemove	where the mouse last moved

Output

write 'hi'	adds HTML to the page
p = write 'fast'	remembers written HTML
p.html 'quick'	changes old text
button 'go', -> fd 10	adds a button with an action
read (n) -> write n*n	adds a text input with an action
t = table 3,5	adds a 3x5 <table>
t.cell(0, 0). text 'aloha'	selects the first cell of the table and sets its text

Sets

g = hatch 20	hatch 20 new turtles
g = $('img')	select all <img> as a set
g.plan (j) -> @fd j * 10	direct the jth turtle to go forward by 10j pixels

Other Objects

$(window)	the visible window
$('p').eq(0)	the first <p> element
$('#zed')	the element with id="zed"

Other Functions

see obj	inspect the value of obj
speed 8	set default speed
rt 90, 50	90 degree right arc of radius 50
tick 5, -> fd 10	go 5 times per second
click -> fd 10	go when clicked
random [3,5,7]	return 3, 5, or 7
random 100	random [0..99]
play 'ceg'	play musical notes

Colors

white	gainsboro	silver	darkgray	gray	dimgray	black
whitesmoke	lightgray	lightcoral	rosybrown	indianred	red	maroon
snow	mistyrose	salmon	orangered	chocolate	brown	darkred
seashell	peachpuff	tomato	darkorange	peru	firebrick	olive
linen	bisque	darksalmon	orange	goldenrod	sienna	darkolivegreen
oldlace	antiquewhite	coral	gold	limegreen	saddlebrown	darkgreen
floralwhite	navajowhite	lightsalmon	darkkhaki	lime	darkgoldenrod	green
cornsilk	blanchedalmond	sandybrown	yellow	mediumseagreen	olivedrab	forestgreen
ivory	papayawhip	burlywood	yellowgreen	springgreen	seagreen	darkslategray
beige	moccasin	tan	chartreuse	mediumspringgreen	lightseagreen	teal
lightyellow	wheat	khaki	lawngreen	aqua	darkturquoise	darkcyan
lightgoldenrodyellow	lemonchiffon	greenyellow	darkseagreen	cyan	deepskyblue	midnightblue
honeydew	palegoldenrod	lightgreen	mediumaquamarine	cadetblue	steelblue	navy
mintcream	palegreen	skyblue	turquoise	dodgerblue	blue	darkblue
azure	aquamarine	lightskyblue	mediumturquoise	lightslategray	blueviolet	mediumblue
lightcyan	paleturquoise	lightsteelblue	cornflowerblue	slategray	darkorchid	darkslateblue
aliceblue	powderblue	thistle	mediumslateblue	royalblue	fuchsia	indigo
ghostwhite	lightblue	plum	mediumpurple	slateblue	magenta	darkviolet
lavender	pink	violet	orchid	mediumorchid	mediumvioletred	purple
lavenderblush	lightpink	hotpink	palevioletred	deeppink	crimson	darkmagenta

Made in the USA
San Bernardino, CA
01 July 2016